WEEKLY WR READER®
EARLY LEARNING LIBRARY

This Is My Story
I Come from Ukraine

by Valerie J. Weber

Reading consultant: Susan Nations, M.Ed., author/literacy coach/
consultant in literacy development

Please visit our web site at: www.garethstevens.com
For a free color catalog describing Weekly Reader® Early Learning Library's list
of high-quality books, call 1-877-445-5824 (USA) or 1-800-387-3178 (Canada).
Weekly Reader® Early Learning Library's fax: (414) 336-0164.

Library of Congress Cataloging-in-Publication Data

Weber, Valerie.
  I come from Ukraine / by Valerie J. Weber.
    p. cm. — (This is my story)
  Includes bibliographical references and index.
    ISBN-10: 0-8368-7238-X — ISBN-13: 978-0-8368-7238-5 (lib. bdg.)
    ISBN-10: 0-8368-7245-2 — ISBN-13: 978-0-8368-7245-3 (softcover)
   1. Ukrainian Americans—Social life and customs—Juvenile literature. 2. Immigrant children—
United States—Juvenile literature. 3. Immigrants—United States—Juvenile literature.
4. Chernivtsi (Ukraine)—Social life and customs—Juvenile literature. 5. Ukraine—Social life and
customs—Juvenile literature. 6. United States—Social life and customs—Juvenile literature. I. Title.
  E184.U5W43   2007
  973'.0491791—dc22   2006018411

This edition first published in 2007 by
Weekly Reader® Early Learning Library
A Member of the WRC Media Family of Companies
330 West Olive Street, Suite 100
Milwaukee, WI 53212 USA

Art direction: Tammy West
Cover design, page layout, and maps: Charlie Dahl

Photography: All photos © John Sibilski Photography, except page 6, courtesy of Serhiy's family

Printed in the United States of America

1 2 3 4 5 6 7 8 9 10 09 08 07 06

Table of Contents

Cover and title page: Our classroom's snake just escaped from its cage. It is funny to watch my teacher trying to jump out of its way.

From a Big Household to a Small One

My name is Serhiy (SER-hay), and I come from a country called Ukraine. I moved to Milwaukee, Wisconsin, in the United States two years ago. I was six years old.

Ukraine and Eastern Europe

BELARUS

RUSSIA

POLAND

SLOVAKIA

UKRAINE

Chernivtsi

HUNGARY

MOLDOVA

ROMANIA

Sea of Azov

Black Sea

Ukraine is in orange on this map.

My family and I come from a small city called Chernivtsi (chir-NIFT-see) in southwestern Ukraine. **Plains** cover much of my country, which makes it good land for farming. We grew a lot of the food we ate. In Ukraine, people often grow their own fruits and vegetables.

5

Our house was on the edge of the city. We had a huge backyard with woods growing behind it. My grandma, grandpa, and aunt lived with us. In Ukraine, people often live with their **extended family**. Grandparents, parents, aunts, uncles, and cousins all stay in the same house.

My family kept pigs, chickens, and rabbits behind our house.

My sister Alexandra was born here. She is six months old now.

My dad moved to the United States first to find a job. My mom and I came to this country two years later. It was hard being apart from my dad for that long. Now the four of us live together in an apartment.

During the day, my dad fixes cars. In the evening, he also helps people when their cars break down on the road.

My mom was a doctor when we lived in Ukraine. Now she is going to school to be a nurse. When she learns English better, she hopes to be a doctor again.

Sometimes I like to watch my dad work on cars.

In Ukraine, I could play in front of my house with lots of kids from the neighborhood. During the day, we played different games all over the neighborhood. We all moved from one person's house to another's.

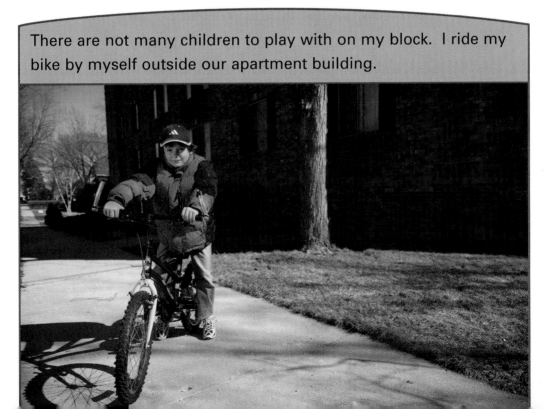

There are not many children to play with on my block. I ride my bike by myself outside our apartment building.

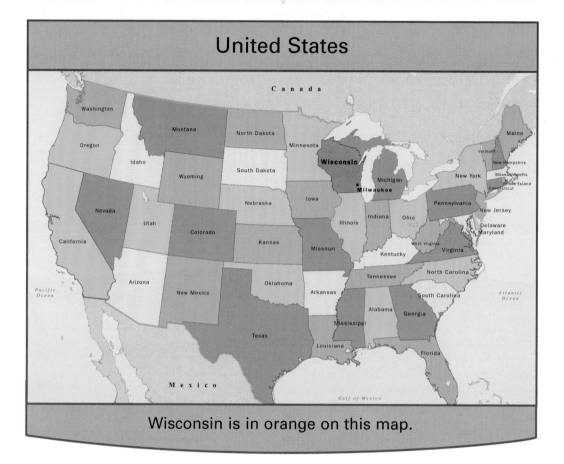

United States

Wisconsin is in orange on this map.

While our home is different here than in Ukraine, the weather is not. Milwaukee's weather is a lot like Ukraine's. Both places have warm summers and cold winters with lots of snow.

I miss my grandparents and my family in Ukraine. We do not have any other **relatives** here. We talk to our family in Ukraine on the phone. For the last two years, I visited them during the summer for two or three months.

Our family photos remind me of the good times I have in Ukraine.

Different Countries, Different Schools

I went to school in Ukraine for kindergarten and a few months of first grade. Then I came to school here.

My school in Ukraine was a few miles from my home. Fewer people in Ukraine have a car than people do in the United States. My family did not have a car, so I took a bus to school.

Here is my school in Milwaukee. I can walk to school here.

I worked on a school project that told about the differences between Ukraine and the United States. In Ukraine, children go to school six days a week. Here, kids attend five days a week. Children in Ukraine also have to do more homework than kids in the United States. They have to know how to multiply and divide by second grade. Here, kids do not learn that kind of math until third grade.

The Ukrainian flag from my project is displayed outside my classroom.

In Ukraine, children from first grade through twelfth grade are all in the same school. We do not have separate middle schools and high schools like they do in the United States. I also think school is harder in Ukraine than in the United States.

Can you find me in my class photo?

This is my regular teacher. I have other teachers for music, social studies, and art.

There is another difference between schools in Ukraine and the United States. In Ukraine, the teacher writes on a chalkboard. In the United States, my teacher uses a marker on a board. Children write in pen in Ukraine, while the kids in my class always use a pencil.

I worked on an **animation** project on a computer for my class. I made cars move across the screen. It took about a month to make it work.

In Ukraine, fewer classrooms have computers than in the United States. Fewer people own their own computers at home, too.

I am showing my animation project to my teacher.

I work hard to spell words correctly in English. English uses a different alphabet than Ukrainian.

I am taking Spanish classes in school now. It is hard to study Spanish when I am still trying to learn English. Sometimes my mother does not understand something in English. I speak English well enough to **translate** for her, though!

In Ukraine, people speak a language called Ukrainian. Many people also speak Russian. I understand Russian when I hear it, but I do not speak it well.

17

Food and Fun

My favorite foods in Ukraine were potatoes, strawberries, and cherries. I like some of the same foods here, but I love peanut butter! We did not have peanut butter in Ukraine.

In Ukraine, we shopped for our food in different stores. We bought vegetables at the fruit and vegetable store and meat at the **butcher**'s shop. We got our bread at a bakery. Here, we go to one big store to buy everything.

Many people eat **borscht** like this in Ukraine. This soup is made from beets.

Sometimes my family plays games together. We also played games in Ukraine. Many of our toys were just the same as the ones here. In both the United States and Ukraine, I play video games on television.

My family used to play this game a lot. Now it is hard to play because my little sister keeps us very busy.

Sometimes I practice kicking a soccer ball on the sidewalk near my apartment building.

Soccer is the most popular sport in Ukraine. Children play soccer in the streets, parks, and playgrounds. My family kicked the ball around whenever we got together in the park. Here, I play soccer at school and with my friends outside my home.

In Ukraine, I used to belong to a **folk dancing** group with other children my age. Here, I take **ballroom dance** classes with my friend Juliya. We know the steps to many kinds of dances. In April of this year, I won the first prize for my age in a state **competition**!

Juliya and I wear special outfits for dancing when we compete.

Glossary

animation — a movie made by moving cartoon figures

ballroom dance — any of a number of dances with set steps for a pair of people

borscht — a hot or cold soup made from beets

butcher — a person who sells meat

competition — a contest

extended family — people's relatives besides their parents, brothers, and sisters

folk dancing — describes dances based on old traditional dances that are often performed in groups

plains — an area of flat countryside covered in grasses and other low plants

relatives — a person's aunts, uncles, grandparents, cousins, and other family members

translate — to change from one language into another language

For More Information

Books

Ukraine. Enchantment of the World (series). Patricia K. Kummer (Children's Press)

Ukraine: A New Independence. Exploring Cultures of the World (series). Rebecca Clay (Benchmark Books)

Ukraine in Pictures. Visual Geographic Series. Jeffrey Zuehlke (Lerner Publications)

Welcome to Ukraine. Welcome to My Country (series). Katherine Brown and Pavel Zemiliansky (Gareth Stevens)

Web Sites

Children of Ukraine
www.chl.kiev.ua/ENG/kart_eserv.html
Click on the "Let Me Introduce" sections to see samples of Ukrainian children's art

Music of Ukraine
www.kochut.co.uk/ukraine.htm
Listen to different traditional Ukrainian songs

Publisher's note to educators and parents: Our editors have carefully reviewed these Web sites to ensure that they are suitable for children. Many Web sites change frequently, however, and we cannot guarantee that a site's future contents will continue to meet our high standards of quality and educational value. Be advised that children should be closely supervised whenever they access the Internet.

Index

About the Author

Valerie Weber lives in Milwaukee, Wisconsin, with her husband and two daughters. She has been writing for children and adults for more than twenty-five years. She is grateful to both her family and friends for their support over that time. She would also like to thank the families who allowed her a glimpse of their lives for this series.